INTRODUCTION

Success Online is very much about matching in all things.

Matching what you offer to what people need.

Matching your passion and enthusiasm to the needs, wants and desires of your customers.

Success is not about being everything to everyone. Neither is it a day dreaming factor.

Success is about being the best you can be and knowing that you have served those who need what you offer to the best of your ability.

Find them through honesty. Serve them with integrity. Listen to them with sincere mind. Grow with them in fear of God.

When you do that, you will have built a legacy, a business that grows strong; survives you and one in which everyone wins.

And that is perhaps the most beautiful thing of all.

Your mind and believe make it possible or impossible.

- ➢ You want to make money but don't know how?
- ➢ You bought products that don't work for you and have left you discouraged?
- ➢ You want to earn commission as others but don't know the platform to use to save your money?
- ➢ Or you are looking for internet eagle to partner with or better still to guide you?

This little book in your hands will help you answer specific questions by channeling you to the right path.

It will help you save money, time and strength and restore confidence in you that will enable you to build from where you stopped.

Which ever form or method you have chosen to run your online business – only thing that matter is you. If you really believe in yourself and are ready to follow the right ways, then your success is sure. You can be that you desired if you wish.

Noble Success

TABLE CONTENT

CHAPTER ONE

SELF - GUIDE

This might be unlike any article you've read because you'll learn different things that really matter before one thinks of **ONLINE MARKETING SUCCESS**. It is the simple truth about doing business online in which ever form – you chose.

- ➢ **Maybe you're seeking the quick, easy way to get where you want to be;**
- ➢ **Maybe you're looking for miracle of this industry;**
- ➢ **Maybe you've seen the success of others and wished to scale through; or**
- ➢ **Maybe you're sick and tired of wasting time; strength and money on products that have left you frustrated with no solution of breaking through the walls of disappointment and regrets, eventually achieve your dreams.**

NOTE: Nature has a way it compels us to go extra miles in achieving what we desire most. It might be through powerful lessons of disappointment. Sometimes we fail to understand this and it becomes problem to us; making some of us clueless in what the real obstacle is, which is standing in our ways. Due to this unknown problem, many of the Online Marketers chase 'Shiny Objects' which pulls them away from the truth they need to succeed.

It has happened to me and I know that many others have tasted it also; and my heart will not be at rest if I fail to let you know this one '**OBSTACLE**' that is standing; starring many especially the NEWBIES in the face; which I know that it is invisible to many who are in this game with the zeal of making it big with a **CLICK**.

What is this ONE OBSTACLE?

Sadly; finding Internet Marketer who really cares and focuses on helping others first is a difficult challenge which has led many into making a choice without their focused mind. Being in this desperate situation, you could spend a large amount of your effort, time and a large amount of your money on those bad ideas, suggestions and recommendations from the **'SELFISH and MEAN'** marketers I call **'INTERNET TURKEYS'**; just to ripe you off your money.

See;

> ➤ I have been PIERCED,
> ➤ I have been PULLED through the thorns,
> ➤ I have been RIPPED off large amount of money and
> ➤ I have been STUNG by these set of internet turkeys.

So, I decided to be the **FLAG** of the survivor that stands to direct others to a clear and honest path, so that they will not fall victim or become captive to these internet Turkeys. I also decided to do this just to save you reading this now a lot of time, money, energy and unnecessary headaches and give you straight forward help that will help you reach your online goals. Note; this can only happen if you sincerely take heed to good advice.

> - **I am not the best writer online,**
> - **I am not the best counselor, neither**
> - **Am I Internet Guru**

But what I bent to do is to shine the light of honesty to the path of those; the Internet Turkeys have laid their invisible snares to destroy their dreams.

No matter the method you have chosen to engage your online business, the only way to succeed is to follow the fundamental truth of this **INDUSTRY** – and the only way you can do this is to find the **TRUE** Internet Eagles.

> - Who are the Internet Eagles?
> - Why the Internet Turkeys?

You don't have to worry; by the time you run through this noble note, you will discover how to find trusted and powerful internet marketers called **INTERNET**

EAGLES that will take you by the hand and walk you through the best method ever; achieving online success. Eventually amazing results you'll see in your business with a fulfilled goals, saving you tons of time and money compared to figuring it out yourself. And also you will be able to understand the wiles of the internet Turkeys to save you from their snares.

Internet Marketing has been the game many have engaged themselves into, often the best and most desired of all the games.

Millions of people have devised different means of wooing others to love their products/services, by putting in all they got. They created channels/funnels to in co-operate others to help in the promotion avenue called Affiliate Program. Through this medium provided many have found their backbones in terms of financial status. These affiliates are now much better than they were in government offices. What a relief from heartbroken situation.

But one ugly truth remains; 'The Presence of Internet Turkeys' which have brought back the heartbreak with their dishonesty. Why turkeys among eagles? A question I have been asking myself for a while, but no answer. Why have some people set up themselves to work against the progress of others? Why would such that detest good things, destroy the good relationship others have built, creating doubt and fears in the heart of many?

The genius have tried all they could to ease the burden of man's hectic works or jobs by introducing the internet marketing avenue, so that people can do their works or jobs, shopping, banking you name it in a minute; all these for the welfare of humanity. Through this wise medium many have been well established in few years compared to many years of running from one bus stop to the other, sleepless night etc.

Everyday Millions surfers round the net in search of business, pleasure and whatever they desire. Twenty five percent of these people are those who seek for an internet marketing platform where they can market their products or services. Five percent of these set of people are those seeking for an internet marketer who will guide them on internet business. Those who have laid their success foundation in a simple format to enable others succeed. Those who love seeing others progress, and are willing to help the newbie in respect of who you are. They are the Internet Marketers whom I call The Internet **EAGLES**. The internet **TURKEYS** are the opposite of these set of marketers.

The Internet Turkey or Chafe seize this opportunity laid by the Eagles to fish in others fishing baskets. They never like seeing others progress, all they care about is themselves. They hove around the net searching for one to devour like hawk hovering around over the hen chicks. Once they notice you're a newbie or a novice to internet marketing, they will present irresistible offer that will subject you to their demands. They will present a One Click **$10,000** offer a day and you yearning to make it will fall woefully.

It will appear to be genuine and honest with a little amount as a sign up fee, definitely if you have not been there and never walked through it; you will fall to it. Just imagine given out $96 as sign-up fee and have a return of **$2, 000 to $10, 000** a day? Whoa! That's hard to resist no matter your knowledge unless you have been through it. You will be given different thing from what they initially introduced to you; presenting a different walk-through just to rip you off the little in your hand. They sometimes promised to run email swaps with you, seeing that you have completed theirs, they will find excuses to deny you access to their own lists. Some of them will not complete the Solo Ads you run in their list, giving you 50% unique clicks and 50% Spam.

I made a purchase on a product; firstly I was told that after I subscribe I will be able to download the software. To be honest, that was what I wanted; but after I signed up I couldn't download the software. I was told to sign in and out anytime I have to use it and different walk-through was given that made me to place a refund order. They forget that genuine and honest means are the best way to market products or services.

Many have quit the game because of the dishonesty of these internet turkeys, but those who are willed never stop searching for the right individual or entity that will finally put them through. Time is the only thing that makes the whole different.

CHAPTER TWO

WHO IS WHO

It is a pity, some of us do not like the step by step process because of the time consumption; and this has made many of us to fall in the snare of the internet turkeys that tell you and I a click for million dollars.

No road to success is clear and smooth. If one must attain success, he must not allow work to intimidate him, and he must be creative. To me; creativity is the closest door to success.

Success is not a quick get access but a gradual and steady process. Success is like the foundation of a building, if it's not solidly laid definitely the whole building will collapse. So success cannot be achieved without a solid foundation, and if you think it will happen, I am sorry to tell you that all your efforts will come to not. For ones foundation to move to its apex must have a concrete and solid structure.

Success is logical not simple and not something you tap your fingers and it is right there. Magic cannot work it out for there is no success except through honest and clear route.

I have been there and have tasted it. That's why I have assured everyone who asked me about internet marketing programs especially the **AFFILIATE** part of it, if it really works. Yes! It works, perfectly well if followed in the right order. Those who persistently follow the clear and honest route will breakthrough. I have been victimized by these set of Internet Turkeys and that is why I have summon up courage to warn you to guard yourself. Don't allow money to be your main focus though is part of the game, rather focus on establishing something that will bring smiles in future; that is the only way you can survive the hurdles of Internet Marketing.

If you really want to know who is who in Internet Marketing, find out through the use of Google or any other search engine you know, type in 'Internet Marketing Forum' then search for the individual name you want to assess. Or better still Google the individual or company you want to assess. E.g. (www.google.com); the name of the person in the search bar) then click on the search.

I am saying this because I don't want you reading this now to fall victim to these set of Internet Turkeys. I have been victimized by these Internet turkeys. I have said it again because the scars are still fresh, through their get rich quick offer. You should understand me, when I said internet marketing turkeys. One thing you must not forget is that; anywhere GOOD exists BAD will not be absent. Think about the programmers who willfully designed this software called Virus and Spy wares; they are all human not spirit so nothing is impossible. To heed not to good advice is the choice of making bad decision. It all depends on you to act wisely.

CHAPTER THREE

POSITIVE ATTITUDE

Don't allow 'I Can't' attitude deny you the wonderful result of your talent. There is nothing impossible to a willed mind. This has been my watch word. And know that creativity, determination and courage are the closest **PAL** to success. The successful always sort different ways to overcome the hurdles of life and never give up when one door shuts. But the failure is orphan to the successful who never finds anything good in others. He believes that he is incapacitated in all things; hoping to get things all the time from people. One thing you should know is, when you trust man and fail to believe in yourself and that you have been made for; you can never be able to stand the disappointment that will emanate from those you trust.

One thing I learnt from all the successful ones I have come across is; 'the never say die attitude they possessed'. This has kept me going even when all measures fail to yield positive results. I kept on believing in myself that I am different from every human being on earth, I have a unique gift and talent that make me different. I have a unique name and I am wonderfully and fearfully made by the Almighty. And I was created for a purpose not by accident; the Creator God who thought of me before my existence had designed unimaginable things to establish me. To be frank these words have kept me going despite all I have been through.

I often cast my mind back to His Words and Promises in Jeremiah 33:3 and it reads; '**Call** unto **me** and **I** will **Answer** thee and **show thee great** and **mighty** things which you know not'. Take note of the words in bold print, do you see the reality of God existence and His presence in your situation? Yes! He has promised me and you great and mighty things if we call. I know too well He will never fail because He is Holy and Faithful.

Why then should I put my trust in man who lives today and tomorrow he is no more? Why then should I believe every word of his when the heart of man is evil and the thoughts continually wicked? Why should I hope in man when everyone is driving to be ahead of others in terms of financial accumulation? No one is satisfied with riches and wealth rather the rich exploit the poor. Millions who called themselves 'failure' are the millions who always say 'I can't' accepting failure before an attempt. If you fail to walk with your legs in your healthy state then how would you be able to run when you're sick? I mean, if you fail to lay the foundation of your success now that you have life; definitely it will be impossible in the future when you're aged. So do not be intimidated by the situation and trials you are facing now but be courageous to move higher.

CHAPTER FOUR

THE TURKEY AND THE EAGLE

I am the type that never let information slip off my hands, head and mind without running through. I subscribed to one hundred different types of Newsletters from different people on internet marketing and I received one thousand in return. That is internet marketing for you.

I was anxious to make it big after going through the stories of few successful internet marketers (the internet marketing Eagles) the likes of **Charlie Page** the owner of **Directory of Ezines, Common Sense Internet Marketing, Follow Up Selling System** and many more; **Anik Singal** a great man to know, **Paul Myers** the owner of **Talkbiz; James Connelly** the owner of **Penny Stock Prophet; Brian Clark** the owner of **Copyblogger, Jimmy Brown** the owner of **Institute, Ryan Deiss the owner of Digital Marketer, Frank Kern** to mention but few.

Like I said earlier, I was very anxious to make it but totally impatient as I wanted to break through the walls of time before time, forgetting that I am a novice and these wonderful people mentioned above and that I couldn't, have been in this business for years. Though I find their newsletters or articles very educative and interesting, which are necessary and the right thing to do if one must succeed online; I felt that step by step process and the walk through are time consuming. I ignored all the information I got from them and went in search of the **quick get rich** set of internet turkeys.

I was happy as I got some and I could not wait to sign up. I went in, paid the fee and was expecting to see money in my bank account the following week or months but believe me; nothing, yes absolutely nothing was seen. You heard me right; I said nothing not even 1 cent was added to my account balance. The worst part of it is; these set of Internet Turkeys will tell you;

➢ You need no experience on Internet marketing,

- ➢ You need no Email list,
- ➢ You need no Banner Ads
- ➢ You need no Social Bookmarking
- ➢ You need no SEO
- ➢ You need no Blogging
- ➢ You need no Traffic at all
- ➢ Not even article writing or content marketing nothing at all you have to do.

All you have to do is sign up and all other things will be done for you. After signing up in that particular program, you will be asked again to open account with their agent who will be your internet broker. Who also will help you in Autopilot to make thousands of dollars a day? They will show you list of huge sum of money belonging to one person. But to be honest, can one succeed Online without some of the listed methods above? I don't think so, because all about Internet Marketing is Traffic; which is the people that surf for things daily on Net.

I kept on signing from one to the other thinking there will be difference, still all returned same results then it was told on me to go back to follow the articles I received from the internet Eagles, which have well-structured method to guide me in building a solid online marketing foundation.

I consulted my mails and the first ever mail I received from these wonderful people was the very one I opened. This mail was from **Charlie Page** and this is what he said;

'A Gift for You

Hi Herbert,

I know you must be surprise receiving this message from me at this moment. It has been a while, I thought of you and how your online business is moving.

I have a gift for you and this gift was the first gift I received from someone. So I thought it will be wise

given it to you too; because I know you will find strength in it.'

Charlie Page.

I had forgetting about this mail for a long time but as I went back to it something **amazing** happened. I was very inquisitive to know what it was. Why have I let this laying for that long without knowing what it is? So what exactly is this gift? I asked.

It takes a Pure Heart to be Honest and Sincere. Integrity is the one thing that makes a man honorable.

CHAPTER FIVE

TAKE YOUR STAND

You might be thinking what exactly the gift was. To be honest with you, this gift worth more than **$100,000** to a willed and noble man. It is said; don't give someone fish rather teach him how to fish.

This gift is **'A Year Of Growing Rich'** by **Napoleon Hills**. The title of this book motivated me to open the attached mail. And I have never cherished a gift the way I did. It was like a million dollar package of gift. I went on reading and applying positively the word. I was inspired beyond my imagination. I was able to write two books based on the motivation I got from this book; **'The Filigree of Success, A Willed Mind'** and **'The Positive Mind Booster, Achiever Of Impossibility' all live in Amazon Kindle**. There is nothing like impossibility if you follow the right part. There is no how you can achieve or attain success if you stand as a stumbling block on others routes; you will never increase rather you will decrease and shrink to foot mat. I have been there, I have been through it; I have tasted and felt the sour that it left in my mouth, believe me when I said; I have been through pain and sufferings, over the lost in the hands of Internet Turkeys. Do not allow the internet marketing turkeys sugar coated words sweep you of your feet. Follow the clear and honest route. I recommend the logical steps if you really want to build a stream of success. The quick get rich never and will never be a solid foundation of success. One's dream can come through in any means either one or different direction; if he is focused. A dream is a desired seed planted by God the Creator in manifestation. One has to take his disadvantages to increase his advantages, take his stumbling blocks to his stepping stones; make people disbelief their wrong option towards him. And take everything around him to build his success. Be creative and use everything you got to build your success foundation. If you're starting as Online

Marketer, be sure to follow the lead of the Internet Eagles.

CHAPTER SIX

THE ROAD TO SUCCESS

One who asks questions never misses his road. So to be on track, ask questions where necessary. This was the aspect I forgot before signing up in those programs.

Go for research on that particular product, the publisher which is the owner to be precise; find out, more within you resources. Watch their walk-through webinars, videos etc. if you have the empowerment you know what I mean {money}, to get full knowledge of what you're about to promote, purchase and advertise.

You must not misunderstand me; not every offer that states click for **$1000** is a fake, I never say that. All I am warning you about is to take precaution not to fall like I did. Be patient with every sign up you did because success is not get all today game.

There are thousands and one site you can get trusted products proven to work, but like I said earlier, patience and determination are required for one to break the walls of hostility. You can get trusted products from **Clickbank, Paydotcom, Rapbank, Zaxaa, Warrior Plus** and many more. One of the places one can get trusted products which are ready to go is **clickbank** especially if you're just starting. There are more sites than what you can think; clickbank platform is much easier than you can imagine. I have to stick to a particular place to fully understand what really works; because inconsistency is the act of uncertainty.

Success is like a licking pool of water; it starts with a drop at a time and consistently in days, weeks, months and years it covers a very large space that hundreds of people can swim across. Be sure to be honest to yourself; don't allow others influence you into attitude that you will regret in future.

You must know that mistakes are part of life which has the positive side of it, if studied very carefully. Never blame anyone for your mistakes or failure but learn and find out the cause; build up from there and never allow that happen again. Let your ideas be transformed into reality and learn generosity. Wake up with a proper start and do whatever your hand finds to do that is good and see whether God will not fulfill His promises in your life.

In the heart of Valor, Generous and Creative Man; lies UNFATHOMABLE SUCCESS

CHAPTER SEVEN

DO AWAY WITH FEAR, WORRY AND DISCOURAGEMENT

Another thing to know is that; every genuine business starts with a slow and steady pace and often drudgery and cumbersome. Do not allow doubt and fears discourage your inner willed mind.

Be bold and brave; learn from the successful ones for they have gone through this road before you.

I will never stop saying or talking about **Charlie Page**. If I am successful today he is one of those that allowed God to use them to motivate me to achieve my dreams. He never stops sending me encouraging articles on which I draw more motivation. I really don't know about others like me in his list; I am highly honored having him as internet marketing mentor.

And to be frank; whenever I am in distress, having the fear that I can't push further, I have to call it a quit.

Then God will touch his heart to send me an encouraging article.

I remembered vividly, on 19th May 2014 precisely Monday of that week. I tried to see how well things are working out but to my surprise, the results put sadness in my entire being. I was contemplating on what to do next when I saw incoming mail, 'from who is this mail coming from now?' I said within me.

Lo and behold; it was from **Charlie Page** My Mentor, I was reluctant to open it. Then I saw the title, **'Your Brain is ATM Machine'**. What does he mean by this? I have to see why my brain is an ATM Machine.

The first sentence my eyes captured was, **'Do you know you can have your own Information Product that can be sold using the internet just for two weeks; yes you heard me right'**. Whoa; I was furious to know this product, the steps and how possible it can be achieved.

My down casted spirit was lifted and I was totally released from the shackles of doubt and fears. I saddled my horse and off I went into study to bring back the stolen treasure of my destiny. I then realized that **WORRY** does the following:

> Destroys your mental focus leaving you clueless

> Accomplishes nothing, and it is a waste of time because nothing will be achieved.

> Health illness and diminished life force

> Robbing one off his natural abilities and talents

> Frustration and confusion about the future and your success journey

> Placing one under his mistakes for years

So, anyone who is **MR KNOW IT ALL** will never move far in his journey; taking a stand to move on, amidst trials is the key to success. You can do it; if I who have been up and down hills several times could stand on my feet to tell you this. What are you waiting for, get into action now, for the future is bright.

CHAPTER EIGHT

YOU HAVE VALUE

Information keeps the life blood of communication afloat, creating ideas and channel of success.

After going through the entire page; I found out that I have been misusing my time. I realized that I have been like a coward who allowed troubles emanating from business discourage him from achieving his goal. I also found out that the positive part of me has been veiled by the negative side making my view on the future uncertain. I tried to rekindle the burning desire of success in me and to consolidate in that I have.

The most interesting part which motivated me most was the section he listed the easy way to publish online and he made mention of Amazon Kindle.

I was moved to pick up the pen to do something better and something that will create the awareness of internet turkeys against the newbie and their method of operation. Though I might not be able to bring to light all the methods they use, because each time they devise different means of running over people on **NET;** when they get to know that their former methods have been revealed publically.

Like I said earlier, if I am successful today, **Charlie Page** is part of it and to be honest he is one of those I can personally recommend to anyone, anytime and anywhere; without looking back. I have never seen him face to face, all have about him is the Pure and honest act of his on everyone. He has no idea that I have chosen him to be my mentor, just like it is said; you don't have to be great or have millions before you can impact positively in peoples' life. Just show that you care, and to tell you the honest true; that's the best. God bless you my mentor and increase your barns.

God can choose anybody, anywhere and anytime to help someone; somewhere and sometimes. It might be you or me. Change is constant and only those that follow it constantly make the best of it. I have more knowledge reading his articles, and that has made me more mature in terms of this game. I can confidently say this because I did take the bold steps of faith, digesting all the information I got; positively getting along with Internet Marketing, so you see there is no impossibility to the optimist.

One thing you should know is; where ever you are in life, know that in one single instant you just need to **DECIDE** what you really want. Fear is the symptom of doubt which is generated by the anxiety of failure. So you must put fear and worry behind you; pick courage and faith for they will guard you, while many that rejected them failed. Build your trust on clear path where doubt will be far, far away from you. Be a soldier; take a hedge against your enemy at night, in the morning your victory song will be heard. Be focused, be determined and worry less.

CHAPTER NINE

MOTIVATE YOURSELF

Another thing I will not forget to let you know is that in every sentences, paragraphs, pages or books; there is one word, sentence, paragraph or page or better still the entire book meant for you either to motivate you to success or to reconstruct your mind positively.

Don't ignore those words that affect you positively; making you see the real person in you. Follow their lead by allowing their manifestation in your lifestyle; if truly you want to succeed.

Napoleon Hills said and I quote **'The person who acts with purpose and a plan attracts Opportunities. Only with definiteness of purpose will you be able to overcome the defeats and adversities that will stand in your way.'**

Success is a learnable skill which needs determination, persistence and focused mind to be acquired.

You're born great, you have value and you're willed. Guard yourself against the internet Turkeys and follow the guide of the successful Ones the Internet Eagles. You'll make it if you stick to the game because the road to success is always under construction; said it again and again.

When you're building a business there will always be people (who are jealous), who will try and tear you and your business down. They do this because they don't have enough confidence in themselves to go after their dreams, so they try to rip yours away from you as well.

However, once you realize this statement is true, all negativity will be washed away, and your overcoming muscles and thoughts will ultimately take over from then on. And often; you'll find yourself laughing in situations where people who aren't prepared for negativity, will actually be crying and thinking "it's all over." Entrepreneurs have overcoming abilities like no one else on the planet, the only way you can get those embedded into your life, is if you go through the fire and come out on the other side without giving up, several times.

Not just once or twice. But if you want to truly make an impact, you'll have to go through the fire more times than you can count and every time the situation will be a little harder, however, overcoming it will feel so much easier because you are now equipped with the overcoming abilities that you once needed. God will never throw at you what you can't handle, you always have the strength to overcome, just trust in what I say here, and I promise it will always be alright as long as you hold on until you push through. In fact, you'll be impressed by the power of your overcoming abilities God has put inside of your spirit.

The Internet Turkeys always say that the old methods are not necessary nowadays because of information overloaded. I do not say no to it, the new methods are good but know that all are built on the foundation of the old method or system. Don't let go of the old neither the new but build on both to survive the hurdles in the game. There is no how you can mark complete success without having complete targeted traffics because that is the soul of internet marketing. If you don't have list you'll depend on other peoples' list to promote your product. Blogging is also another method, then bringing in the Ads methods, all these are from the starting of this game which are the old methods of marketing.

Internet marketing is all about presenting, advertising or selling companies products in the best possible ways. And that's why Affiliate program is the best and easiest way to start online business. You should bear in mind that it will never be that easy when starting but with time you'll breakthrough.

NOTE: There's no impossibilities to the willed and determined man and nothing like give up in his dictionary

CHAPTER TEN

BUILD YOUR SUCCESS

Try to do things on your own; don't always expect the finished goods. Learn to blog; write content or articles and the rest of them because there you find the joy of who you really are. Yes I mean it. I don't know if you have checked your post and see that people actually viewed, click or comment on it. To me it gives me joy that someone, somewhere not known to me could view my post; that means everyone has something to offer weather good or bad. Why not turn these writings into something that will gear up your success? Good advice is very scarce rejecting one will be very costly to afford another time.

Secondly, these things are things you'll fall back on in future, and then all the so called new methods are everywhere, people will no longer request for them anymore; find out who you really are through the above listed method of advertising. For that which you created; is the pride in your success.

Don't allow what people say discourage you; you can do it and now is the time. If you can teach a child how to hold the spoon to eat; you can teach someone somewhere how to live a normal life; or how to solve a particular problem by picking up your pen, your voice, or video medium. One thing you must not do is to force yourself on it; if you really want to put down your ideas for others to benefit from.

Take your time and allow the ideas to flow through; write down every piece of it until you have run out of words, for whatever you put down at that moment is good. If you're so good on internet, you can help someone somewhere by writing down the steps to take to find program or information on mobile or desktop through search keywords. You can also write on how to download or install software, how to design website etc. There is no information that is a waste as long as it puts one person through. Like I said in previous pages above, after going through the mail **Charlie Page** sent to me titled **'Your Brain Is ATM Machine'**; which the content encouraged me to write down that I know; that someone somewhere needs it, I went in study to write the little about **HTML Programming and now is LIVE** in Amazon Kindles 'Titled, **HTML PRO – APPS, WEB DEVELOPMENT'**.

'There are many lonely hours we toil in our craft behind closed doors. It is essentially invisible. No one celebrates it (in fact, we are probably teased and mocked by some friends and family; and even our inner critic tends to fire off heckle as soon as we begin). No one pays for it (in fact, it costs us time with no promise of return). It often seems we are all by ourselves with only the murmurs of critics and our doubts as company. But in time, as we pursue mastery and effectiveness; the crowds often begin to swarm and money begins to surge. If you continue to quietly sow your seed, even in tears and loneliness, eventually you will reap a public harvest greater than you can imagine. This is the essence of Invisible Leadership; Psalm 126:6 is the blueprint'.

I so much love the writings of Napoleon Hills and everywhere I go or things I do; I often use them as my backbone besides the Word of God. The Great Writer says and I quote:

'A genius is simply one who has taken full possession of his own mind and directed it toward objectives of his own choosing, without permitting outside influences to discourage or mislead him. Such is a famous man who turned adversity into advantage, who overcame great obstacles to become rich and famous. He is the successful person who converted stumbling block into stepping stone'. What else can I say besides these powerful motivational words from the great writer to ginger you up? If you fail to take the will power built in you by God, no one will ever do that for you. Dare to get more then dare to be more.

CHAPTER ELEVEN

AUTHORITY

We must understand the affiliate marketing is a really business, not something to 'try'. Like I said earlier, the successful ones who were persistent and focused have laid great platform for others who will come after them, people like you and I to succeed. And they have carefully put down the easy stair case in step by step format to enable those that are ready, attain success; with little or no effort.

If you fail to take the first bold step, definitely; the second step will be too difficult and heavy to be lifted. Start with the little in your hand, head or pocket in due time, your effort will be rewarded. No one is perfect and only when you accept and admit that you need help; and then you will definitely get one.

People reject information and they miss much than they can imagine. Do not reject information in its entirety, what you should and ought to reject is the negative side of it. I don't reject information especially documented ones and I tell you the truth, I build my world around it. I know that I am not perfect and my knowledge section is not filled; so I will continue to download more and more information to evolve with time. Information they said makes the world go round. If you believe this then you have something that someone, somewhere ought to hear or know.

Do you know that in a day the human brain can convey seventy thousand thoughts? Something that weighs 3pds; there're more in the brain than you can view physically. So why don't you make use of it positively to save yourself from danger of failure lying ahead.

Our minds are living libraries, there are much wonderful words from the books up there, turn all into one standard motivational book. All you have in mind stay till death, so there is no delete button. Reconstruct your mind positively to produce success because only the positive and honest mind achieves it. **Prov. 2:1-4**

Your thought is exact manifestation of who you're. Negative minded person will never have positive thought in life because all in his library is negative books making him pessimistic in all he engaged in.

Whatever you conveyed into your mind will be translated into action, so you ought to lock your mind against negative thoughts if you really want to attain success.

Negative thought is like foaming sea, which is trackless. How can you make head way without the right and clear path? The decision is yours to make; I know too from experience that affiliate marketing can create a full time income and requires little or no overhead or technical skills. It's a fact; some truth is hard to hear. Sometimes it's easier to let our ears be tickled by the sites that promise easy riches, promise "one click" results; and promise **50,000** visitors a day. The sites that promise a six figure income this quarter! We know in our hearts those methods don't work but still we buy and try exactly what I said earlier happened to me. If **$97** product could give you **$1000** a day, believe me there is no way the Turkeys will allow that amount for Instant Access to it. You have to sanitize yourself from that.

Intelligence is the product of Creativity which is the best link to Success. With a focused mind and perseverance, Success is not far from your reach. Don't let Fear hold you to captivity, take the bold step now to take up that you desire no matter what people say, don't give in to their discourage word. Learn to be yourself. There are thousand and one marketing platform online trusted you can take up now.

You've done it before and you can do it now. See the positive possibilities.

CHAPTER TWELVE

HONESTY

Redirect the substantial energy of your frustration and turn it into positive, effective, unstoppable determination. You have to learn the rules of the game. And then you have to play better than anyone else. Only those who dare to fail greatly; can ever achieve greatly. Motivation is the key you owe yourself to Succeed. **'A generous man will himself be blessed, for he shares his food with the poor. A good name is better or more desirable than great riches. To be esteemed is better than silver or gold. Rich and poor have this in common: The Lord is the Maker of them all. A prudent Man sees danger and takes refuge, but the simple keep going and suffer for it. Humility and the Fear of the Lord bring wealth and honor and life. Prov 22:1-4';**

This happens to those that are faithful, who are trustworthy that play this game with honesty. The success stories of the brave and willed.

Affiliate success stories, platforms and steps to excel in this field are what I bent on and will bring to light the means to avoid failure on this game. An Optimist is a willed man who believes that impossibility doesn't exist; exactly the mind I want you to have.

Information is the live blood that sets the **NET** in motion; positive ones are the only success channel which is desired by the positive thinker to break the walls of failure. Evaluate your resources before embarking on a project.

➢ What is your goal?
➢ Set your goals,
➢ Respect your dreams and goals,
➢ Set more time to achieve your goals
➢ Have a burning desire to achieve your goals
➢ Your goals most dominate your thinking, if you must achieve them.
➢ Your goals should be definite.

NOTE: You will never attain specific level without total believe to yourself.

You must invest before reaping but in a good platform that will guarantee you that you desire. Follow the honest route; don't be afraid in your quest. Make constantly; changes to your goals to fit in the time.

Work with this; to meet you goal:

➢ Set a specific time.

➢ Write down six things u have to achieve in a year.

➢ Target short goals and pursue it with honesty.

➢ Always note the dotted place. Where you failed or had difficulties.

➢ Do not engage yourself in white elephant project.

➢ The greatest path to success is in God's Words. Philippians. 4:8

CHAPTER THIRTEEN

PASSION

This will do you a lot good than harm if you heed to it. if you have be victimized by the internet Turkeys, bury the pains and move on, never dig it whenever you see the scars; exactly what I did to shut the door of my mind against it. But if you have not been ripped off by these groups, learn from others mistakes to save your pocket. It is said that, 'Curative is costly than Preventive'; and it is best to protect oneself from danger than to cry 'had I know'.

I don't have the will power, money, or knowledge to purchase good advice and that is the reason I never ignore one; but when I do, I pay dearly.

Do you really have passion on this game, Internet Marketing?

Do you really have fun doing it?

If you do, you're on course but if you don't; definitely you have to sit back to analyze your interest and wants to know what really makes you fulfilled.

You must have **PASSION** on what you engaged in because:

- ➤ It is the force that moves an optimist to conquer failure.
- ➤ It is the spirit that revives the soul of a determined man to never give up in what he believes
- ➤ It is a rocket that fires the positive thinker to be outstanding among his competitors.
- ➤ It is a mining of knowledge to the willed mind.

To survive, you must be honest to yourself. Don't do things because others are doing it, if you don't have passion for that; though it is good to try those things one have fears on. Allow your heart to direct you to the joy your life desired but one thing you will never forget to do all the time is **'PRAYER'**. Always communicate with God and allow Him speak to you.

You're the only one that will tell others how much you can bear to succeed; and also the only one that will show others how your success story should be written. Like I said earlier; sometimes, it is good for someone to do what he fears; it might be the best thing that happened to him.

I have been telling you what an honest and positive thinker should do to overcome failure online and other related businesses. But I have not really explained who an Affiliate or Affiliate marketing is; which is the first step for everyone who has no product of his own online uses to build up to the next level.

WHO IS AN AFFILIATE?

Affiliate is a person who promotes; advertise or sell products of a company and in turn receives commission for his services.

Many companies have their affiliate platforms and their melt out commissions. Some keep to their promise and some fail. It takes Eagle's eyes to see these companies who pretend to be Eagle while they are Turkey. I have explained the little you ought to know and my advice is also listed above, follow the honest people; find out **who is who** before committing your money.

NOTE: Some companies also require their affiliate to sign up with a token while some allows free sign up, depending on what they really promote. But if you are an affiliate who wants to succeed online, and you don't have the economical empowerment; follow the simple format **blogging** though it will not be that fast for you to see returns. Patience and determination are needed if you must succeed using free sign up method. You must also have enough content to back up you promotional tools like your affiliate link, banners and videos.

Rich Content in simple format will surely produce result, because every 'Ads' out there is all about Content and its format. What makes your content presentable that will attract visitors? It must be helpful which has a specific purpose that will lead to trust, and when you have gotten the trust of people; your 'Ads' will generate positive results. So you have to be honest in whatever you're doing. I told you early about one of the Internet Marketing Gurus and Internet Eagle who has helped me all the way, **Charlie Page**. He is a wonderful person I can recommend anyone to. I will equally put my money on the line about his products; they are success platform everyone who wants to succeed should involve in.

CHAPTER FOURTEEN

WHO TO WORK WITH

When your conscious focus on the various elements that produce positive mind in the peace will, you will move along much quicker in whatever you want to do than hammering out a lot of words with no direction. When you do this often, holding on to the positive thoughts; your awareness of the structure of the game and the pacing of your understanding will improve in noticeable ways in very little time. It will make you look as intelligent as you are, command more respect and credibility for your thinking and make it easier for you to connect with others. Sometimes when everything seems no way forward, all you have is your dreams which keep you going. Hang and tie them around your neck and move on. The best way to create your own list as affiliate is to create your own products.

You can only do this by following the step by step format of this business; through the help of the honest men and women in this industry. Learning from them is the best way, and also they will guide you in every step of the way.

This I must leave you with:

The Internet Turkeys, some of them use names like:

- ➤ Admin
- ➤ Support Member
- ➤ Support Team
- ➤ Auto Pilot, Auto Software, Auto Cash etc.
- ➤ Account Team
- ➤ Account Service
- ➤ Account Management
- ➤ Papal Account
- ➤ Marketing Support Team
- ➤ Payment Confirmation and
- ➤ Many More I can't remember now

So, be careful how you fall to their wiles.

The Headlines of their emails are often in this manner:

- ➤ Please Confirm Your Account
- ➤ Important – Concerning Your Account
- ➤ Bonus – Activated – Collect Now
- ➤ Your Attention Is Required (URGENT)

- ➢ **RE: Your Account Update**
- ➢ **Two Words: FREE CASH**
- ➢ **Your Direct Access To Your Account**
- ➢ **New And Hot Software Generating $30K/Day**
- ➢ **Receive $500 – Absolutely Free**
- ➢ **Your Software Download Now**
- ➢ **Your Account Has Been Credited**
- ➢ **Your Secret Link To Your Account**
- ➢ **Congratulations! Your FREE Software Is Ready**
- ➢ **And millions I can't LIST**

Take a look at these headlines or titles of the emails once again, can anyone who wants to build a solid foundation online, gain something positive? Do they have anything one can learn from? All they keep saying **ACCOUNT, MONEY, ACCOUNT, and MONEY. Why?** Because they have no idea of what it takes to build an online passive/stream income. All they want is to take from you for their daily needs.

Now let me **LIST** Few Emails from the Internet Eagles so that you can compare and contrast, see to which is more **EDUCATIVE** and **INFORMATIVE**.

These from The Internet Eagles

- ➢ Headline Fundamental To Online Marketing
- ➢ Six Parts Of Solo Ads That Work

- The Cure For Confusion – Online Marketing
- How To Write Content That Produce Clicks And Conversion
- Free And Paid Methods Of Ads
- List Building And How To Convert Them To Customers
- Article Marketing Does It Really Work?
- How To Promote Your Niche
- Affiliate Marketing – Does It Work?
- The Best Way To Use Your Blog To Build Your List
- The Best way of Using Adword On Keyword/Market Research
- And Many More I can't LIST

NOTE: Each of these mails have step by step **CONTENT** format on what the title is and their real names are stated clear. So tell me now, who I should work with?

Building ones success online or anywhere else requires:

- Honesty
- Integrity
- Humility
- Love
- Creativity
- Determination
- Persistency/Consistency
- Self – Guide

- ➢ Winning Strategy and
- ➢ Good Rapport

Simply follow the Proven step by step of the Internet Eagles and see how successful your online business will be. Be honest to yourself and let your vision be realized through the honest path. Hold onto your value and worth, Integrity pays much more than you can imagination. You're bound to success and you'll succeed, steady connected to the right channel.

CHAPTER FIFTEEN

FIRST THING FIRST

There are lots of things to learn when one is starting any form of business, not only on Online Marketing. The fundamental **TRUTH** of such; is the **KEY** to success in any of these businesses and that is why I said earlier that, anyone that wants to succeed in whatever he or she is doing must be keen to **INFORMATION**.

Because you cannot hit a target that is invisible to you, aimless shot means no target. And you cannot conceive what your mind has no knowledge of. So your expectations will be met base on the level of your knowledge, the more you **RESEARCH** and **DIGEST** the information within your reach, the more you will **GROW** in knowledge of the business you're in.

Note also, if you must have good work; you have to practice and practice and practice. Let me use myself for example; if you noticed the previous pages you read, you must have heard my said that **'I built my world around INFORMATION'**. Exactly, I am the type that always desire having a book **AUTHORED** by me after reading various articles on:

- ➢ Stage Presentation
- ➢ Podcasts
- ➢ Webinars
- ➢ And all other forms of Marketing Online

If I fail **READING/WATCHING/LISTENING** to these things listed above, how can I write or explain to someone who needs to know what I have learnt? Could there be a magic that will work it out for me without writing and writing about these things to have the full knowledge I desire? How can I achieve my goals or dreams without practicing? That is why I will never forget this saying, **'A Talent Without Practice Is Heading To Its Demise'**.

You must do all you desire in right direction knowing where you're coming and where you're going; I said this again and again. If not, you will never get to your destination, 'meaning your goals will not be achieved'.

In every **ADVERT**, there are things that matter most and which helps one to succeed in his campaign. And Online Marketing is all about creating the awareness of your product/service to millions who surfer around the net. Some might have a specific product in mind or some might not. But the most important part of this is how to attract them to that you're selling or adverting.

First thing which matters most here is the **HEADLINE or TITLE** of your Ad. Headline is fundamental to Online Marketing. Headlines are one of the keys to successful Online marketing campaigns. It should be the magnetic force that pulls your prospects or readers. It might be solo Ad which is specific or targeted; it might be content marketing which also goes with the headline, article marketing, blogging or social methods. Whichever form you chose to run your Ads boils down to the same thing. Now how do you know **HEADLINE or TITLE** that will attract clicks and conversions?

There are different types of headlines depending on your choice of usage. And I personally chose to name them in this way:

> ➢ Social Fact Headlines
> ➢ Menace Headlines
> ➢ Reward Headlines

Each one of the above headlines has a method that suits it and it must correspond with the body of your campaign. Many use different headlines with different body contents to deceive the reader just like the **INTERNET TURKEYS**. Note; honesty and integrity are the best way to keep your list members or your readers' faithful making them trust every word you passed across. The killing tricks behind the successful pulling traffic on social media are better and interesting **HEADLINES**. Sure everyone wants something that will attract them without second thought and that is the work of an Interesting and better **HEADLINES.**

This will also keep the conversation alive as your customers, prospects and partners on this media will engage themselves finding out more from you. But some of the sites like **TWITTER** and **FACEBOOK** are full of information which I call information **CHANNELS**. Mostly we often encourage clicks to our campaign site or landing page which requires a constant updates with a content that will generate much clicks. A content that generates clicks is not necessary to be a page; it might be a content of Ten words, Eight words or Three lines sentences and so forth.

You must also know that status **UPDATE** of some of these media loses value in no time. Especially Twitter update loses it value in few days, so if it did not generate click within the time posted and few days, it will never get clicks because twitter updates has short life span. So building a perfect platform on **HEADLINE** writing puts you ahead of others. And be sure to go back to your headlines over and over before posting. Testing the headlines are also the best way to know the one that gets more attention of people and your are advised to use it over and over again.

Having well knowledge of **HEADLINE** writing will make you stand out in terms of:

➢ Social Page Headlines
➢ Blog Post Titles
➢ In – Person Sales Communication
➢ Book or Report Titles
➢ Presentation Titles
➢ And many more

By this you will have people to say **YES** to your 'call to action' **(CTA)**; more and more will be attracted to your niche with a genuine purpose of patronizing your products or services. Note that 'A great **WRITER** is known by the **TITLE or HEADLINE** of his book/article.

Let us see the above listed **HEADLINE METHODOLOGY** to enable you understand where each falls.

CHAPTER SIXTEEN

HEADLINE METHODOLOGY

SOCIAL FACT HEADLINES – An excellent marketing incorporates social proof base on the choice people make that resulted others marketing the same choice.

Human being generally loves and wants what is said to be popular, in the sense of belonging to the happening group. So bringing in a headline that informs them about others been ahead in usage or attendance; they will eventually want to know why. Especially with a well known area with influential people; then will the post attract more people to click to find out more about the information.

- Let's take for instance; one of the Mega Cities in your country as a venue where Indigence or particular set of people will have a get together on a particular date (i.e. why 1000's of Lagosians and State Security will gather in Sheraton on 27th May)
- Let's consider the name of well known people; one of the ministers in your country. What he does after work or his diet or better still Lifestyle

(i.e. What Senator Nziribe Reads At Night). People will be more anxious to find out the hind secret and then you have just gotten their attention.

- Let's also consider the wants of people either on net or in their homes (i.e. The New Cure to Malaria Everyone Is Talking About/The Latest Smart Phone Everyone Is Talking About)
- The headlines has an Interesting Signal that attracts people to take action, just like I said; to find out the hidden secret is always what people are willing to do.

MENACE HEADLINES – This method of headline is the headline to put people in anxious mode and create a fear that makes the reader desire to know why. People fear failure more than that of success, so any word that causes doubt and fear is employed here to get the attention of people. Menace headlines like the following create that burning desire to see the secret behind them.

- Why You Will Not Succeed In This......
- Why Animal Flesh Maybe Dangerous To Your Health ......
- If You Fail To Get This Now, You'll Hate Yourself In Future ...

66

These headlines are sure to get clicks because people want to know the solution to their failure, with a menace headline; the call to action will be **YES** all the way.

REWARD HEADLINES – This method also brings people to take action because of the benefits and promises listed which will be offered if they take action.

People love listening to what brings gain and they desire to hear them or see them often. So telling them about your company's products with the benefits motivates the **YES** response.

- How To Create A Website You'll Be Proud Of Within 10 Minutes
- How To Install WordPress In Your WebSite With Few Clicks
- Sixteen Steps To Convert Traffic To Cash
- Simple Ways Of Saving Your Dog From Ounce

With these Headlines people will always want more from you if truly you live up to expectation by giving them exactly what your headline says. All about good and quality Ads boils down to the way your **HONESTY AND INTEGRITY** are seen in all you do. You need to be faithful to yourself if truly you want the trust of others. Success is always there, but focused mind is needed to direct your desires to it. And you must also know that the **HEADLINE** is the manifestation of the **BODY/CONTENT** of you Ads in sentence. Like I said earlier, don't use a different headline with a different content in the name of making money or deceiving people to click or visit your website. You can only deceive them clicking to find out what you have but you won't force them to buy from you, so be honest to gain peoples' trust.

Now follow the lead and work with the Internet Eagles.

Ignore the glittering messages of the Internet Turkey.

Plant your Success on a solid and proven platform if you really want to be happy with this Industry.

You can make it if you believe it.

To your SUCCESS ONLINE!!!!